# A Journey to the Heart of Evangelism

# A Journey to the Heart of Evangelism

*Discover How to Share Your Faith from Your Heart
—You DO Have a Story!*

JANICE KEATS

RESOURCE *Publications* · Eugene, Oregon

A JOURNEY TO THE HEART OF EVANGELISM
Discover How to Share *Your* Faith from *Your* Heart—You DO Have a Story!

Copyright © 2009 Janice Keats. All rights reserved. Except for brief quotations in critical publications or reviews, no part of this book may be reproduced in any manner without prior written permission from the publisher. Write: Permissions, Wipf and Stock Publishers, 199 W. 8th Ave., Suite 3, Eugene, OR 97401.

Unless otherwise stated, Scripture quotations are from the New International Version.

Resource Publications
An Imprint of Wipf and Stock Publishers
199 W. 8th Ave., Suite 3
Eugene, OR 97401

www.wipfandstock.com

ISBN 13: 978-1-60608-850-0

Manufactured in the U.S.A.

gkeats@eastlink.ca
www.inscribe.org/janicekeats

## Contents

*Foreword* vii

*Preface* ix

*Acknowledgements* xi

*Introduction* xiii

1. The Call—Can God Use Me? 1
2. Duty Calls 6
3. The Message Revealed 24
4. The Results Are In 30
5. Reaching Your G.O.A.L.S. 38

# Foreword

WHAT a great way to help us think through what we believe (or "if we believe!") in Jesus as our Lord and Savior. Jan Keats has written a thought-provoking, soul-blessing book, helping us to think through the fundamentals of our faith.

We met in extraordinary circumstances, 9/11 having just happened. I found myself in Gambo, Newfoundland at a Salvation Army church along with the passengers from Flight 929 United! I was attempting to return to Chicago from Russia when the twin towers went down. We were cared for as only the army can, for six days till we traveled back to the States. During those days I watched Jan live out these principles of life in Christ and for Christ among us.

Touching on principles of the Christian life Jan makes the application unmistakable. I like the format as we can take the learning in bite-sized pieces and digest it at our own pace and in our own time. Surely with the world in the turmoil it is in we should get serious about what we believe and why we believe it! The time is short; the days are evil.

I have a theory that people the world over have "not rejected Jesus, they haven't had a chance to hear the Gospel and respond." Let's give them this chance. After all someone gave it to us! This book shows us how.

Jill Briscoe<br>
Author and Bible teacher

## Preface

Have you ever felt stifled when asked, "Tell me why I should become a Christian" or "What difference does Christianity make?"

Are you really prepared to answer? Think about it; how would you respond?

I have been faced with that particular challenge. I was asked by my pastor to take his place for an interview with a medical student as he had another meeting to attend. What began as a secular conversation about the community turned into a challenge to be ready in all situations. I surprised myself; I was prepared. I had taken my Bible into the office with me to prepare for my next visit with an elderly lady—not realizing that I would need that actual reference before me. The Scripture that I had selected to read was just what I needed to share with the student.

The medical student with whom I had a meeting that day was Chantal. We engaged in a wonderful conversation about my community. After about ten minutes or so, she caught me off guard and changed the conversation. "I like a good challenge," she said, as she stretched her hands back over her head, leaning back in the office chair. "Tell me why I should follow Jesus."

The question came out of the blue, and was totally unexpected. After a very quick, under-the-breath prayer, I began to share my faith story. I replied by saying, "Well, the best way to answer your question is to share my faith experience with you." And I did. I began with how I discovered Christ, with God guiding my thoughts and steps. I shared how my life was before I met Christ and my need to surrender to the One who was knocking on my heart's door.

I pray that you will find these exercises helpful as you learn and discover for yourself that sharing your faith story is not a frightening experience, but a joy as you draw closer to Him! When Chantal left, I felt satisfied that I was able to share God's message of love. I have learned through the Scriptures that Jesus went to various places spreading the Good News. He taught in synagogues and sat with believers and nonbelievers alike to share the Gospel.

# Acknowledgements

THE TOPIC of evangelism has been my passion and continues to be the main focus of my Christian journey. My goal is to share God's love with others so that people can learn the Gospel message and grow in His grace.

Many people have been influential in my spiritual growth over the years. To all of my Bible study friends at my home church, The Salvation Army Citadel, Gambo, Newfoundland, I dedicate this book. Together, we have shared and grown in God's grace, through prayer, Bible study, and fellowship. To the previous pastors there who still share the same passion: Calvin Fudge, who nurtured me as a new believer in Christ, and Wayne Loveless, who exemplifies the true compassion of Christ, thank you.

I would like to acknowledge the support I received from my friend Joanna Mallory. She has been and continues to be a great encourager in my writing career.

Finally, I would like to acknowledge Patricia Thomas, who took time out of her busy schedule to accommodate me in preparing the final stages of this book.

# Introduction

Are there still people out there with the desire to reach the lost? Is evangelism ongoing in the lives of Christians? Do you ever wonder what the following questions really mean?

- Who is responsible to reach the lost?
- Have I surrendered to God?
- What is my role as a Christian?
- How do I respond to the call of evangelism?
- How can I follow the example of Jesus?

This book on evangelism was prepared to help you become better equipped to build relationships so that others will come to know Christ as Savior. " . . . discipling them to become mature Christians attaining to the whole measure of the fullness of Christ" (Eph 4:13).

We will examine these questions to find easy and simple answers to help gain a better understanding of knowing God and His will intimately. Then with the help of the Holy Spirit, we will be ready to reach out to the harvest, to help win the lost for Him.

At the end of this book there is a chart to help reveal your personal walk with God, and your faith story. Also included is a step-by-step plan to help you prepare and share your faith story more comfortably. In conclusion, you will find a progress chart to use when you launch out to seek those lost sheep that God places in your path.

What is evangelism all about? Let's examine the Scriptures and discover the answers.

1

## The Call—Can God Use Me?

- ✳ God may call you *on the spot*.
- ✳ God may call you *in a dream*.
- ✳ God may call you *in a still voice*.
- ✳ God will call you because *you are chosen*.
- ✳ God has given *the open call*.

### EXPLORING THE SCRIPTURES

THE FOLLOWING Scriptures pertain to these calls from God. At the end of each point, write down or underline some words or phrases that stand out to you. Also, write out your thoughts how each person may have reacted to God's call.

a) On the Spot—Matthew 4:18–19

Two brothers were fishing on a lake, and Jesus walked by and called out to them, "Come, follow me," Jesus said, "and I will make you fishers of men."

> *Little did they know they were going to drop their nets that day to become the first disciples. They left their normal routine of life behind to obey Jesus. What do you suppose their thoughts were as they*

*dropped their nets and walked away to meet up with Jesus?*

---

b) In a Dream—Genesis 28:12–13

Jacob had a dream of a stairway from the earth to heaven, with angels ascending and descending. Above the ladder stood the Lord, "and He said: 'I am the Lord, the God of your father Abraham and the God of Isaac. I will give you and your descendants the land on which you are lying.'"

*When Jacob awoke from his sleep, he realized it was a genuine encounter with God. Do you think it was difficult to determine whether or not the dream was real?* (See Gen 28:16)

---

c) In a Still Voice—Luke 24:15–17, 32

Two men were going to a village called Emmaus. They were talking with each other about the day's events, the delightful news of Jesus' resurrection. "As they talked and discussed these things with each other, Jesus Himself came up and walked along with them; but they were kept from recognizing Him. He asked them, 'What are you discussing together as you walk along?' They stood still, their faces downcast" (vv. 15–17).

*They talked about the events of the past three days and when Jesus dined with them that evening their eyes were opened and they knew it was Jesus who was with them all along.*

They asked each other, "Were not our hearts burning within us while He talked with us on the road and opened the scriptures to us?" (v. 32).

*Why do you suppose, they were kept from recognizing Jesus during those moments? Do you suppose they did not understand the resurrection of Jesus? Were their hearts not open? What do you think?*

_____

_____

_____

_____

d) You are Chosen—Joshua 1:2, 5

Following the death of Moses, God chose Joshua to continue the challenge of leading His people across the Jordan River and into the Promised Land. He said, "Now then you and all these people get ready to cross the Jordan River into the land I am about to give to them—to the Israelites" (v. 2).

> *God had a command for Joshua. He was the chosen leader to take Moses's place. All of God's promises accompanied Joshua's commission. What would God have done if Joshua refused to obey Him? How would Joshua have felt had he deliberately disobeyed God? What would have happened to God's people?*

"As I was with Moses, so I will be with you; I will never leave you nor forsake you" (v. 5).

> *How do you think Joshua felt at that moment? After all Joshua was about to take the lead and wait upon God for the Promised Land. (See also Acts 9:15)*

_____

_____

_____

_____

e) The Open Call—John 7:37b–39

At the feast, Jesus extended an open invitation to all who were thirsty to come to Him. "If anyone is thirsty, let him come to me and drink. Whoever believes in me, as the Scripture has said, streams of living water will flow from within him. By this He meant the Spirit, whom those who believed in Him were later to receive. Up to that time the Spirit had not yet been given, since Jesus had not yet been glorified."

> *This was announced at the last, and greatest day of the feast. Then Jesus resumed His ministry. It was an opportunity to offer the free gift of life through His*

*imminent death. What do you think the buzz was among the crowd that day?*

_____

_____

_____

_____

## 2

# Duty Calls

- ❈ "Evangelism is for those who are called."
- ❈ "God didn't give me the gift of evangelism."
- ❈ "There are already enough people in the church who do that work."
- ❈ "I don't know how to evangelize."

Have you heard these statements before? Do you fit into any of these categories?

### EXPLORING THE CHRISTIAN DUTY

EXPLORE THIS checklist to make sure you're lined up with God's expectations. Look up each of the following Scripture references and give careful consideration to them. Are you living up to God's standards as the text describes? Write down a few thoughts about how you feel God is speaking to you through these verses.

1. Have you given up everything and placed God first? (Luke 14:33)

_____

2. Do you have compassion for the lost? (Luke 15:4)

3. Are you devoted to one master only? (Luke 16:13)

4. Is the Kingdom of God within you? (Luke 17:21)

5. Have you accepted Jesus' testimony? (John 3:11)

6. Do you acknowledge Jesus in all your ways? (Prov 3:5–6)

7. Do you believe that Jesus is the Savior of the world? (John 4:42)

8. Do you have a relationship with Jesus? (John 8:47)

9. Do you love others as Jesus would love? (John 13:34)

10. Do you proclaim Jesus fearlessly? (John 12:42)

11. Are you excited about the Gospel message? (Acts 2:42–47)

12. Do you believe the validity of the Gospel message? (John 8:26)

---

## THE DUTY

Explore the following Scripture references and summarize in your own words what you think you ought to be doing in sharing God's message.

> "I tell you the truth, anyone who has faith in me will do what I have been *doing* . . . " (John 14:12a).

---

---

> "The world must learn that I love the Father and that I *do* exactly what my Father has commanded me" (John 14:31).

---

---

> "This is to my Father's glory, that you *bear* much fruit, showing yourselves to be my disciples" (John 15:8).

---

---

*Doing* is imperative in spreading the Gospel message. "Do not merely listen to the Word, and so deceive yourselves. *Do* what it says" (Jas 1:22).

---

---

## Learning To Follow

Have you ever asked yourself, "How *do* I follow Jesus?" Have you ever struggled with the thought, "*How can God possibly use me to benefit His Kingdom*?" Matthew 4 gives a vivid description of the first disciples to be called by Jesus. Imagine yourself and a friend out fishing on a lake, having a relaxing time, and when you return to the shore, suddenly you hear Jesus calling out to you saying, "Come follow me, and I will make you fishers of men" (Mark 1:17). Wow! Do you stand there frozen, with the fishing gear still in your hand, in awe of "*Who*" just called you? Or do you hastily leave everything behind to join the Master?

Imagine what Simon and Andrew must have been thinking after they walked a few miles with Jesus and turned back to see the shore in the distance. They dropped everything to follow Jesus. Their gear may have been still visible. Their catch of fish may very well have been still jumping in their buckets on the rocky shore. Do you suppose it was their last glimpse of life as they knew it? Perhaps it was.

Their lives were dedicated in the safekeeping of their Master. Life had taken on new meaning and purpose for them. They traveled, they learned from their great teacher, and they shared the good news of eternal life with everyone they met. They were mission bound! It wasn't all glory and dance though. The Gospels record many hardships and trials Jesus and the disciples and many followers faced.

There was one particular occasion along the journey where they stopped and some wondered if the mission was too difficult for them to continue. They complained that Jesus' teachings were too difficult to follow. Consequently, some departed. Let's journey with them for a moment.

After Jesus had chosen His twelve disciples, they, along with many followers, traveled to various towns and villages sharing the good news of eternal life. Jesus spent most of His time with them, training and preparing them for His imminent trial and death that was soon going to take place.

After awhile something strange began to happen. Many who followed Jesus began to question His teachings. "On hearing it, many of His disciples said, 'This is a hard teaching. Who can accept it?' Aware that His disciples were grumbling about this, Jesus said to them, 'Does this offend you? What if you see the Son of Man ascend to where he was before? The Spirit gives life; the flesh counts for nothing. The words I have spoken to you are Spirit and they are life'" (John 6:60–63).

> *I wonder what the thoughts were of those who continued along, through the trial, and the crucifixion, to actually witness the glory of the ascension?*

Imagine that moment in time when the journey paused. Can you just hear Jesus saying, "Friends, are you with me or not? Don't you believe in the Gospel message and in *me*? You've followed me this far and you have difficulty trusting me?"

Why would some discontinue with the Gospel mission? Was the message really that difficult to follow, as they said?

*Duty Calls* 11

Was the hardship of the message the real reason that caused some to turn and walk away? Jesus, knowing full well what was happening said, "Yet there are some of you who do not believe" (John 6:64).

Aha! Some folks were becoming disgruntled, but Jesus had known who didn't believe His teachings from the very beginning of the journey and who would betray Him (John 6:64b).

Jesus turned to the twelve disciples and asked, "You do not want to leave too, do you?" Simon Peter answered him, "Lord, to whom shall we go? You have the words of eternal life. We believe and know that you are the Holy One of God" (John 6:67–69).

We discover that there were people who had mixed feelings about the mission that Jesus was leading. Is that how Christians feel today? Has your life changed for the Gospel mission? Did you join the force wholeheartedly knowing that there would be some hardships? Did you look back with the yearning to go back? Did you hesitate along with the doubters who found the teachings too difficult to comprehend and practice? While many may have turned back, still many more followed and continued in the journey.

There were plenty of fish to be caught in the deep sea, but not by the disciples. They had nothing to worry about; their *catch* was men—not fish. They had a new path set before them. But it was with Jesus, the One who chose them to be the future spokesmen for the sake of the Kingdom of God. They held firmly to the Gospel truth. The disciples' faith proved they were worthy of all Jesus had promised them.

God promises provision, protection, and guidance as we stand our ground for Him. May we firmly grasp His truths so that we will never be tempted to walk back to where we once were, but instead, to continue with Him holding firmly to His hand. In this way, God will effectively use us to be His partner and friend in mission, until the day of completion—as He has declared! Jesus reassures the crowd that His way is the true way. Even though many deserted Jesus and His teachings, the journey continued as Jesus and His many followers, and the chosen twelve, followed.

Stop here for a moment. Reflect upon Jesus' teachings and ask yourself...

- ❋ "Is this too difficult for me?"
- ❋ "Do I believe in all He says?"
- ❋ "Am I willing to follow His teachings?"
- ❋ "Can I really apply His teachings and continue on the journey?"
- ❋ "Did I *truly* believe in the first place?"

Now ask yourself, if you really believe that Jesus is the Holy One of God? (See John 6:69; also Isa 43:10–11) Have you ever stopped in the fork of the road (in the spiritual sense) and wondered what direction you should take? Write down your thoughts.

_____

_____

_____

_____

## Following in Obedience

The disciples asked, "What must we do to do the works God requires?" Jesus answered, "The work of God is this: To believe in the One he has sent" (John 6:28–29).

Let's look at *willingness* as a requirement:

Do you remember, as a child, when one of your parents asked you to run an errand and you didn't feel like doing it at the time? Perhaps you were having too much fun with your friends, or you were about to play basketball, or hang out at the mall. I'm sure that you did what was asked out of respect and obedience, *and then ran off in haste afterwards*. I remember my kids doing just that!

Is willingness a prerequisite to believing? Is an unwilling *working* heart a deterrent to believing? What work does God expect us to do anyway? In His answer to the disciples, He said it is to *believe in God*. Perhaps if He had continued the dialogue He would have asked, "Are you willing to do my work?"

So they asked Him, "What miraculous sign then will you give that we may see it and believe you? What will you do? Our forefathers ate the manna in the desert; as it is written: 'He gave them bread from heaven to eat.' Jesus said to them, 'I tell you the truth, it is not Moses who has given you the bread from heaven, but it is my Father who gives you the true bread from heaven. For the bread of God is He who comes down from heaven and gives life to the world'" (John 6:30–33).

So, there's the difference. . . . Allow me to pose the question this way: Do you believe that God gives life to the world? Are you willing to believe that God is the true bread of life who came to give life to the world? If the willingness is there, then there must also be motivation to carry out His will! There must be a beginning to every journey!

When the disciples finally believed that Jesus was speaking the truth, they asked for the *true* bread of life. Jesus said, "I am the bread of life." At that moment, He gave the invitation to come and dine with Him. ". . . whoever comes to me I will never drive away" (John 6:37b).

To do the work God requires, is to believe in the true God, to be willing to follow the true God, and to accept the invitation to dine with the true God . . . *from start to finish!* "For my Father's will is that everyone who looks to the Son and believes in Him shall have eternal life, and I will raise him up at the last day!" (John 6:40).

The work of God is this: to believe in Jesus. We are to carry on with the teachings of Jesus. He instructed His disciples to proclaim the message. The written Word is for all to heed and obtain knowledge. Obedience to Him is expected and required. Jesus knows the temptations and trials that will come our way. But our faith and trust must be complete, in Him.

But wait . . . Jesus said, "If they persecuted me they will persecute you also. If they obeyed my teaching, they will obey yours also. They will treat you this way because of my name, for they do not know the One who sent me" (John 15:20–21).

We can do the work of God because He gives us the power to do it.

*They Will Obey Our Teachings Also! Hallelujah!*

So, we can rely on God's power to step out into our communities with faith, and assurance, despite the threat of persecution.

What do the above Scriptures imply?

- ✹ We must be willing to do His work.
- ✹ We must believe He will work with us.
- ✹ We must believe in the Trinity of Christ.
- ✹ We must remain strong in faith despite persecution.
- ✹ We must be obedient and honor His Word.
- ✹ We must believe if we decide to follow.
- ✹ We must allow God to prepare us for the work.

## WE CANNOT DO GOD'S WORK *WITHOUT* THE HELP OF GOD

Can Christians live without the power of God? How does God's power work within us? Let's study the following Scripture passage to find out.

> "I pray that out of His glorious riches He may strengthen you with power through His Spirit in your inner being, so that Christ may dwell in your hearts through faith. And I pray that you, being rooted and established in love may have power, together with all the saints, to grasp how wide and long and high and deep is the love of Christ, and to know this love that surpasses knowledge—that you may be filled to the measure of all the fullness of God" (Eph 3:16–19).

This is what we discover from these Scripture verses:

- ❋ He gave us the power to understand His love, so that we might follow Him.
- ❋ He gave us the power of inner strength to live for Him through the Holy Spirit.
- ❋ He gives us the power to understand His love and the inner strength to live for Him on a daily basis.

Even though we do not understand the depth of His love, He still gives us His power to be filled with the fullness of life, and that power comes from God!

### We have a duty to work the fields

Jesus appointed the seventy-two disciples to go ahead of Him in pairs to every town (Luke 10:1). *Why?* Jesus clearly indicated the need for many workers to reap the harvest.

> He told them, "The harvest is plentiful but the workers are few. Ask the Lord of the harvest, therefore, to send out workers into His harvest field" (Luke 10:2).

Let's consider the following points:

- ❋ Jesus' workers forged ahead to prepare the people for the arrival of Jesus.
- ❋ The workers went ahead in groups of two.
- ❋ Jesus was training His workers for the work that was present but also for future ministries.
- ❋ Jesus needed the help and efforts of all believers.
- ❋ There still is a great work to do after Jesus overcame the world.

✸ The field is the place in which we live; the parameters are within reach.

Jesus sent His workers out as lambs among wolves. The Lord's work wasn't necessarily an easy feat. But the message was clear, Jesus gave this instruction, "When you enter a town and are welcomed, eat what is set before you. Heal the sick who are there and tell them, 'The Kingdom of God is near you.' But when you enter a town and are not welcomed, go into the streets and say, 'Even the dust of your town that sticks to our feet we wipe off against you. Yet be sure of this: The Kingdom of God is near'" (Luke 10:8–11).

Many rejected the message of love. Jesus, however, promised His workers strength for the journey and power to heal in His name, and when the seventy-two returned they were filled with joy and exclaimed, "Lord, even the demons submit to us in your name" (Luke 10:17).

It may not have been a glorious journey for them but they were surely filled with the joy and power of the Lord!

## WE HAVE A DUTY TO FORGIVE

Jesus taught us to forgive one another. When people sin against one another or if anyone sins against God, we are to rebuke the sin and forgive the sinner. Jesus said to His disciples, "Things that cause people to sin are bound to come, but woe to that person through whom they come" (Luke 17:1).

> "If your brother sins, rebuke him, and if he repents, forgive him. If he sins against you seven times a day, and seven times comes back to you and says, 'I repent,' forgive him" (Luke 17:3–4). (See also John 20:23)

Oftentimes, dealing with emotions is difficult. When people say hurtful things to others they tend to dwell on the unkind words. Those unkind words can spin off into months or perhaps years if forgiveness is not willing to play a part in reconciliation.

Let's examine what is learned from the above Scriptures:

- Sin is still evident and will attempt to destroy relationships.
- Jesus told us to be cautious when temptation comes.
- We must help our fellow Christians to overcome sinful habits.
- We must allow our fellow Christians to seek forgiveness.
- Keeping sin at bay is our duty!
- Forgiving those who sin against us gives both parties a clear conscience.

If we are to be followers of Christ and abide by His example then we ought to learn from His Word. Since He is a compassionate and an all-forgiving God, then we, His children, ought to be also. "Therefore as God's chosen people, holy and dearly loved, clothe yourselves with compassion, kindness, humility, gentleness and patience. Bear with each other and forgive whatever grievances you may have against one another. Forgive as the Lord forgave you" (Col 3:12–13).

If a friend sins against you and causes great emotional pain and suffering, then decides to ask forgiveness, how should you react? Would you forgive your friend? Why or why not? What would result either way? Would you be able to take God at his Word and example? Would you be able to continue to live with the emotional suffering if you didn't trust God to help you?

Take some time to write your thoughts.

_____

_____

_____

_____

Something to think about:
- Can we have compassion and not a forgiving heart?
- Can we have humility and not a forgiving heart?
- Can we have gentleness and not a forgiving heart?
- Can we hold grievances, and at the same time display compassion and patience?

What do you think?

_____

_____

_____

_____

_____

In other words, can we, God's chosen people, hold on to grievances and be like Christ? Of course not, but there is a reconciliation path to become like Christ. Each of us can have a forgiving heart like His! Forgive as the Lord forgave you. There is grace enough to be made whole. There is grace enough to replace the burden of an unforgiving heart into a joy that can be restored! There is freedom in repentance and forgiveness!

## WE HAVE A DUTY TO PERSUADE MEN EVERYWHERE TO REPENT AND BE SAVED

Take notice of the following Scriptures pertaining to the solid assurances from God:

> "For the Son of man came to seek and save that which was lost" (Luke 19:10).

> "Repentance and forgiveness will be preached in His name to all nations . . . " (Luke 24:47).

> "Salvation is found in no one else, for there is no other name under heaven given to men by which we must be saved" (Acts 4:12).

> "The Father loves the Son and has placed everything in His hands. Whoever believes in the Son has eternal life" (John 3:35–36a).

> "With great power the apostles continued to testify to the resurrection of the Lord Jesus, and much grace was upon them all" (Acts 4:33).

What do these Scriptures imply?

- ✺ The message is repentance, forgiveness, and salvation.
- ✺ The One we preach is the crucified Christ.
- ✺ God gives power to the workers.

- ✺ Jesus came to save the lost.
- ✺ The message is also the resurrected Christ.
- ✺ Jesus is the only way to heaven.
- ✺ Jesus ought to be preached everywhere.

## Personal Evaluation

Take some time to evaluate your thoughts and pray about them. Perhaps you may prefer to write down some weak areas in your life right now.

1. Is there anything that stands in the way of being free to pursue God's will?

　

　

2. Is forgiveness difficult?

　

　

3. Is trusting God difficult?

　

　

4. Are personal struggles preventing you from being fruitful for God? What are they?

5. Is fear an obstacle in embarking on fieldwork?

_____

_____

6. Is someone else an obstacle?

_____

_____

7. Do you feel that all you can be is a follower? Why or why not?

_____

_____

8. Is there an idol that comes first in your life?

_____

_____

The following chart may help you discover your strengths and weaknesses. Check the appropriate level where you feel you are right now in your Christian journey. Take your time and study each category and check where you feel you are in your faith.

| Category | Weak | Coasting | Ambitious | Strong |
|---|---|---|---|---|
| **Sure of Salvation** (Wholehearted decision made.) | Lack knowledge and skills. | Little effort, God is still working on me. | Strong desire, but haven't reached full potential. | Using spiritual gifts, and bearing fruit for God. |
| **Obedient** (Willing to listen and follow God's instruction.) | | | | |
| **Praying for Lost Souls** (Concerned for the lost.) | | | | |
| **Bold and Confident** (Risk-taker.) | | | | |
| **Bible Study** (Personal or group attendance.) | | | | |
| **Bearing fruit** (Love, joy, peace, patience, kindness, goodness, faithfulness, gentleness, self-control Gal 5:22–23.) | | | | |
| **Witnessing** (Sharing Christ and the salvation message.) | | | | |

# 3

# The Message Revealed

## EXPLORING THE MESSAGE

"For I have come down from heaven not to do my will but to do the will of Him who sent me" (John 6:38).

"He who sent me is reliable, and what I have heard from Him I tell the world" (John 8:26).

"I have come into the world as a light so that no one who believes in me should stay in darkness" (John 12:46).

"But the world must learn that I love the Father and that I do exactly what my Father has commanded me" (John 14:31).

"And through Him to reconcile to Himself all things, whether things on earth or things in heaven, by making peace through His blood, shed on the cross" (Col 1:20).

The Lord has come . . .

The Lord has come to do the Father's will . . .

The Lord has come to proclaim and offer to the world eternal life . . .

The Lord has come to rescue His people from darkness . . .

The Lord has come to bring peace through His blood, shed on the cross.

## The Message is Love

Jesus continually taught His disciples holiness, love, obedience, and truth, exemplifying His true examples. When it came time to leave, Jesus promised to send the Holy Spirit to replace Him until He returned once again. The Holy Spirit was given to reign in their lives.

> "No, the Father Himself loves you because you have loved me and have believed that I came from God" (John 16:27).

> "As the Father has loved me, so have I loved you. Now remain in my love" (John 15: 9).

### THE FINAL COMMAND

> "My command is this: Love each other as I have loved you" (John 15:12).

> "Greater love has no one than this, that He laid down His life for His friends" (John 15:13).

#### Do we really get it?

Jesus' love is so great for humankind that He actually laid down His life so that abundant and eternal life could be made available to mankind. There's the ever-so-sensitive second part in this command: Love each other! Understanding God's love for the individual is perhaps slightly easier to decipher than to be able to have an unconditional love for those who persecute, treat one another unfairly, even cruelly, or unjustly.

When faced with criticism, and anger, and ungodliness, and persecution, God's Word says we are to love and pray for the perpetrators, " . . . that you may be sons of your Father in heaven" (Matt 5:44–45), meaning that God will help in times of trial and as a result, we, God's people, remain honest and true to the Father.

## ONE ON ONE LOVING RELATIONSHIP

The disciples were trained in righteousness and faithfulness, and to be true examples of Christ. What do you suppose happened to Peter when testing time came? Let's explore the character of Peter in John 21.

Jesus asked Peter point blank, "Simon son of John, do you truly love me more than these?"

"Yes, Lord," he said, "You know that I love you."

Jesus said, "Feed my lambs."

In all, Jesus asked Peter three times if he loved Him. Peter was perplexed that He was asking him that question. Peter had previously denied knowing Jesus during His time of trial, and Peter was sorry for denouncing Jesus. Of course Jesus knew that Peter loved Him; Jesus was simply attempting to grasp Peter's full attention. It became a spiritual encounter—a meeting one to one, face to face. Jesus' simple, yet profound command to Peter was, "Follow me!" Peter later became one of the greatest spokespersons to edify the Gospel.

Jesus expressed compassion to those who needed physical healing, as illustrated by His encounters with lepers. Leprosy was a disease that had a tremendous impact on the community. The disease was particularly wretched. It scarred and disfigured human features, and lepers were known as the untouchables. Such a leper came to Jesus and begged Him on his knees, "If you are willing, you can make me clean."

Filled with compassion, Jesus reached out His hand and touched the man.

"I am willing," He said. "Be clean."

"Immediately the leprosy left him and he was cured" (Mark 1: 40–42).

Of course Jesus healed the man. But He did more; He touched the man with His hands. That man mattered to God. That was love without question!

Jesus' love extended far beyond one community. Jesus expressed His Love to others in many ways. Jesus has shown His love through touching, healing, speaking, praying, socializing, and most of all, dying. Jesus began His ministry preaching to the poor and restoring sight to the blind—in the physical sense as well as the spiritual. Crowds of people came to Him because they heard about the great things He was able to do and had already done. Jesus healed many along the journey. It was out of this act of love that the Gospel was spreading.

Why would a man named Jesus spend so much time and work so hard to heal and help people and tell them about heaven? The Scripture says in Luke 4:18, "The spirit of the Lord is on me because He has anointed me to preach good news to the poor."

Why? Because God loves everyone so much that He sent His son into this world to be our Savior. Jesus said in Luke 4:43–44, "'I must preach the good news of the kingdom of God to the other towns also, because that is why I was sent.' And He kept on preaching in the synagogues of Judea."

Jesus sent His disciples to continue in the journey of sharing God's love to all the nations. Jesus called people to be preachers, teachers, encouragers, leaders, and workers to keep on preaching where we are or where we are called. So if we are to be like Christ then we ought to carry on the Gospel mission with love. What is love? Love is an intentional expression of action. First John 3:16 says, "This is how we know what love is: Jesus Christ laid down His life for us. And we ought to lay down our lives for our brothers."

Jesus understood sorrow, and once again as we explore the love of Jesus we learn that He was filled with compassion and heartfelt empathy. In Luke 7 we learn that when Jesus traveled through a town called Nain, He witnessed a dead body being carried out through the town gate. This dead man was an only son of a widow. "When the Lord saw her, His heart went out to her and He said, 'Don't cry.' Then He went up and touched the coffin, and those carrying it stood still. He said, 'Young man. I say to you, get up!' The dead man sat up and began to talk, and Jesus gave him back to his mother. They were all filled with awe and praised God. 'A great prophet has appeared among us,' they said. 'God has come to help His people.' This news spread throughout Judea and the surrounding country" (Luke 7:13–17).

Jesus witnessed many of these diseases and sicknesses and sorrow. He ministered to all He encountered throughout His travels. He was their healer, friend, brother, and compassionate Father. This good news about Jesus traveled very far among respective communities where He ministered and taught. He stayed and He listened.

# 4

## The Results Are In

### EXPLORING THE RESULTS

WHAT IS happening in Jerusalem? (See Acts 1) The mission continues . . . Following Jesus' ascension into heaven, the disciples waited for the promised Holy Spirit. Jesus told them to stay in Jerusalem and wait for the gift that the Father had promised (Acts 1:4).

Indeed, the Holy Spirit came and rested upon them. "Suddenly a sound like the blowing of a violent wind came from heaven and filled the whole house where they were sitting. They saw what seemed to be tongues of fire that separated and came to rest on each of them. All of them were filled with the Holy Spirit and began to speak in other tongues as the spirit enabled them" (Acts 2:2–4).

As a result of the wind and the different native languages that were being spoken by the disciples, the crowd gathered together in bewilderment. This was the beginning of the many wonderful, yet challenging, opportunities to share the Gospel message. God gave the disciples the power to speak with authority and persuasive words. What resulted were many converts and a new gathering of saints.

## The Message is Going Forth

So, we've looked at the message, *and* the mission. The present-future goal was to win new converts and endeavor to train new converts in righteousness and truth. The disciples set out with optimism to reach out in love with boldness for the sake of Christ.

Peter addressed the crowd saying, "Men of Israel, listen to this: Jesus of Nazareth was a man accredited by God to you by miracles, wonders, and signs, which God did among you through Him, as you yourselves know. This man was handed over to you by God's set purpose and foreknowledge; and you, with the help of the wicked men, put Him to death by nailing Him to the cross" (Acts 2:22–23).

Bewildered, perplexed, curious, and now God-fearing, the crowd listened and paid attention to Peter's gospel message: "Repent and be baptized every one of you, in the name of Jesus Christ, for the forgiveness of your sins. And you will receive the gift of the Holy Spirit. The promise is for you, your children and for all who are far off—for all whom the Lord will call" (Acts 2:38–39).

Those who *accepted* his message were baptized.

Peter's first converts numbered three thousand.

## Let's Peek Into God's Transforming Power... and Paul's Earnest Desires

The Apostle Paul was transformed completely through Christ's power and grace. The transformation caused his earnest desire to *sacrifice self's desires* for the Gospel, in order that others may be persuaded to follow Jesus. He stated in

1 Corinthians 9:22, "To the weak I became weak, to win the weak. I have become all things to all men so that by all possible means I might save some."

Paul's desire to serve and fulfill the burning and longing in his heart was evident in that he was willing to drive beyond human efforts and rely on his God-given strength to "become all things to all men." In other words, to walk to where, or to whom, the Lord leads, for the sake of the Gospel mission.

A strong desire to follow God's path leads to bountiful blessings and joys. Paul's mission wasn't to fulfill self or attain personal goals. No! He said, "I do all this for the sake of the Gospel, that I may share in its blessings" (1 Cor 9:23). To paraphrase, God is first and foremost; plenteous blessings always follow.

## The Servant

" . . . as servants of God we commend ourselves in every way; in great endurance, in troubles, in hardships and distresses" (2 Cor 6:4). Paul held strongly to the Gospel truth. He was firm and steadfast in his duty to God. Yes, there were hardships of every sort in the ongoing battle, but was the mission worth suffering for? Paul says, unquestionably, that it was. He was, "known, yet regarded as unknown; dying and yet he lived on; beaten and not killed; sorrowful and yet rejoicing; poor yet making many rich; having nothing and yet possessing everything" (2 Cor 6:9–10).

On the flipside, if Paul had no desire to fulfill God's will for his life, he wouldn't have this testimony. He couldn't "say" or "do" for the sake of the salvation of men. Furthermore, he would not be able to withstand beatings, imprisonments, riots, sleepless nights, or hunger. A passion to become all things to all men causes all hardships and distresses to become secondary, perhaps insignificant. Following in Christ's footsteps is first and foremost. Walking in God's path is the safest and most trusted direction.

To have nothing in this world, and to choose to determinedly follow the path of the Savior results in possessing everything, everything that is needed to obtain a fulfilling life. If so, what is the driving force?

Love! Paul stated, "Christ's love compels us," which means without Christ's love, we operate on fumes! Fire is the fuel, the Holy Spirit, to keep us strong, afloat, and earnest to do His will. Whether we are weak or strong, new to the faith, or live in an urban or rural community, we need to depend on the Holy Spirit.

## Learning from the Scriptures—Biblical Accounts of God's Impact on the Community

Let's journey with Jesus as He leads the way . . .

### THE WOMAN AT THE WELL—JOHN 4:4-26

As Jesus was passing through Samaria He stopped at a well and along came a woman to draw water. Jesus asked the woman to give Him a drink. The woman was surprised that a Jew would even associate with a Samaritan. Jesus knew she was confused and replied, "If you knew the gift of God and who it is that asks you for a drink, you would have asked Him and He would have given you living water" (v. 10).

Jesus began conversing with her, explaining that the true living water comes from God, so she asked Him, "Sir give me this water so that I won't get thirsty and have to keep coming here to draw water" (v. 15). Before long He told her everything about her life. In their brief and final moments Jesus declared, "I who speak to you am He" (John 4:26). She was so amazed that when she went back to her hometown, she told many people whom she had met. As a result many believed in Him because of her testimony (v. 39).

ZACCHAEUS—LUKE 19:1–10

Once again Jesus was about to pass through another community, Jericho, in continuation of His ministry. The chief tax collector, Zacchaeus, came along. He ran ahead of the crowd to see Jesus. Because he was so short, he decided to climb a tree for a better view. To the amazement of the tax collector, Jesus called him down from the tree and together they went to the home of Zacchaeus to have dinner and spend some time together. It didn't go over well with some of the people who were also waiting to see Jesus pass by. They muttered among themselves, saying, "He has gone to be the guest of a 'sinner'" (v. 7). Jesus' purpose prevailed however, and Zacchaeus became a changed man. Jesus declared, "Today salvation has come to this house, because this man too, is a son of Abraham" (v. 9).

SAUL ALSO KNOWN AS PAUL—ACTS 9:1–19Here we have an account of the person who was the least likely to be converted. Saul was a persecutor of the church. He even went out diligently seeking those who belonged to the way of God, to have them thrown in prison for their faith. "Meanwhile Saul was still breathing out murderous threats against the Lord's disciples, when he went to the high priest and asked for letters to the synagogues in Damascus so that if he found any there who belonged to the Way, whether men or women, he might take them as prisoners to Jerusalem" (vv. 1–2).

Something miraculous occurred along the way that surprised even Saul. God interrupted Saul's plans to hunt down and persecute His people and called out and questioned him in an audible voice, "Saul, Saul, why do you persecute me?" (v. 4). A light shone around Saul and as a result he became blinded and even though he did not know what was happening he asked, "Who are you, Lord?" (v. 5).

Here is a firsthand witness of a genuine encounter with the powerful Almighty. Little did Saul realize how powerful God actually was. Imagine the strong, defiling, persecutor of the church was now, perhaps, a trembling Saul. In a blind state Saul was led into Damascus and upon receiving his sight he began to learn and preach the Gospel. "At once he began to preach in the synagogues that Jesus is the Son of God" (v. 20). And yet another account of a transformed life!

### The Jailer—Acts 16:22-34

A powerful earthquake awakened the jailer. It wasn't a natural disaster, however; it was divine intervention. Paul and Silas were imprisoned for their faith and for proclaiming the Gospel mission. "About midnight Paul and Silas were praying and singing hymns to God and the other prisoners were

*The Results Are In* 37

listening to them. Suddenly there was such a powerful earthquake that the foundations of the prison were shaken. At once all the prison doors flew open, and everybody's chains came loose" (vv. 25–26).

It was the jailer's duty to keep watch of the prisoners and now he feared for his life. He thought the prisoners had escaped so he drew his sword to kill himself but then he heard the voice of Paul shouting, "Don't harm yourself! We are all here!" (v. 28).

The jailer realized that he needed to believe in the One who performed this miraculous event. He ran to Paul and Silas and asked, "'Sirs, what must I do to be saved?' They replied, 'Believe in the Lord Jesus and you will be saved—you and your household'" (vv. 30–31).

The jailer did become a believer, as did his whole family. The jailer invited Paul and Silas to his home and took care of their wounds and fed them. The jailer's fear was turned into joy when he believed in Jesus. And remember . . . when Paul and Silas were praying and singing in the prison, everyone could hear them. This is how fellow believers have an impact and influence upon others!

### The Centurion—Luke 7:1–10

The centurion's servant was about to die. What could anyone do to prevent imminent death? Only Jesus could restore life. The centurion heard about Jesus, and His teachings, so he sent some of his elders to go to Jesus and ask Him to come and heal the man. When they encountered Jesus they pleaded with Him to come and do something to save the servant from death. Their plea was admirable because the servant was deserving of life because of all he had done (v. 4).

If the centurion was so concerned about his servant, why didn't he go and search for Jesus himself? He declared he wasn't worthy enough. He felt that he didn't deserve to have Jesus as a guest under his roof so he sent some of his friends out to meet Jesus, to tell Him not to bother to come. "He was not far from the house when the centurion sent friends to say to Him: 'Lord, don't trouble yourself, for I do not deserve to have you come under my roof. That is why I did not even consider myself worthy to come to you. But say the word and my servant will be healed'" (vv. 6–7).

Jesus thought otherwise... when the friends of the centurion continued relaying the centurion's message of how he had authority over the soldiers and servants under his care, Jesus recognized a man of faith. In fact, Jesus turned and faced the crowd of followers behind Him and proclaimed, "I tell you, I have not found such great faith even in Israel" (v. 9b).

Jesus was amazed! Did He heal the servant? "Then the men who had been sent returned to the house and found the servant well" (v. 10).

Was the centurion worthy of such a request? Yes, of course he was worthy; he acted on faith. He summoned the elders to initially *go and look for Jesus* while his servant lay helpless and dying. Jesus responded out of love and compassion. Isn't that just like Jesus?

# 5

# Reaching Your G.O.A.L.S.

## G.O.A.L.S.—GO OUT AND LABOR FOR SOULS

JESUS WENT to various places spreading the Good News. He taught in synagogues and sat with the multitudes and He also sat one on one, each time, sharing the Gospel.

Preparing your testimony—Consider these points:

First write down some key points about your relationship with Christ. This exercise will help you prepare a simple synopsis of your personal story to share with people. In the next step, we will actually write a testimony or faith story!

1. What is my story?

   *What do you believe? Know whom you believe in and why. Write out the simple facts of your faith.*

   _____

   _____

   _____

   _____

## A JOURNEY TO THE HEART OF EVANGELISM

2. What was my life like before Christ?

   *Analyze your attitude, your disposition, and your lifestyle.*

   _____

   _____

   _____

3. What changed after I found Christ?

   *Was there satisfaction? Was there joy? Was there a difference?*

   _____

   _____

   _____

4. How has it affected my family? My work?

   *Did they acknowledge a positive change in you? Are you happier? Are you at peace?*

   _____

   _____

   _____

5. What is my involvement in church?

    *Are you actively involved in any way in church? Are you excited to learn the Bible? Do you express Christian love to others?*

    _____

    _____

    _____

6. Compare and contrast worldly joy and Christian joy.

    *Write some noticeable differences between the old ways and the new.*

    _____

    _____

    _____

7. Compare worldly goals and eternal life.

    *What is the new focus? What are your goals as you live out the new path that Christ has set before you?*

    _____

    _____

    _____

8. Compare worldly contentment and spiritual contentment.

    *Describe how life takes on a new meaning.*

    _____

    _____

    _____

9. Compare the comfort the Holy Spirit brings versus human comfort.

    *Write down your experience of the presence of the Holy Spirit in your life. How has the Holy Spirit enabled you to get through some tough circumstances?*

    _____

    _____

    _____

10. Share newly formed friendships.

    *Have you noticed the difference in the warmth and friendliness of people? Since your transformation have you noticed yourself becoming attracted to the faith you see in your peers? How about yourself? Do you welcome spiritual advice?*

    _____

    _____

    _____

Reaching Your G.O.A.L.S. 43

11. If you were raised in a Christian home and accepted Jesus at a young age, share how God has been faithful to you over the years.

   *Has God helped you and honored your prayers? Write some examples.*

   _____

   _____

   _____

12. Think about some of the struggles you may have had in making a decision to follow Christ. Perhaps you had to make certain changes in your life, such as refraining from former habitual desires or having to deal with peer pressure.

   *What helped you overcome the struggle? Was it a result of prayer or a friend who supported you?*

   _____

   _____

   _____

13. What encouragement have you received?

   *Are fellow Christians encouraging? Has anyone actually shared their faith story with you?*

   _____

   _____

   _____

14. Is there a spiritual mentor in your Christian life?

> *Is there someone who stands out to you that truly expresses trust and faith in God? Is there someone who stands by you who offers support and serves as a spiritual mentor? Do you see God's love through him/her?*

_____

_____

_____

15. What has kept you faithful to God?

> *What keeps you interested in discovering more of God? Have you developed a good Bible study habit?*

_____

_____

_____

The Next Step:

Review all your answers. You may find that together they have a natural flow, just like typical storylines. Based on your answers to these questions your faith story could be something like the sample that follows.

## A Sample Personal Faith Story

I didn't have a deep-rooted spiritual upbringing like some people I know. My early life was great and I was blessed with wonderful parents and siblings. From that traditional vantage point my goals were simple and I really didn't have a need for church in my life. I attended college and settled down with my family.

After awhile my life seemed empty. I began a search to find the something that was missing. A friend invited me to church one Sunday and it wasn't long before I was attending on a regular basis. Suddenly, I realized I was on a quest for inner peace. Some time passed and then came my moment of decision. One particular Sunday evening during a church service I felt God's presence prompting me. His presence flooded my soul. That evening I surrendered to God and experienced a newfound joy!

I discovered for myself that the peace God offers is genuine. I could not doubt God's power and love any longer. I've been telling people wherever I go about God's amazing grace. I have become more involved in church activities and meeting new friends. I know the Christian life is not easy, but I am more content and at peace than ever before. Even my co-workers have noticed and commented about the change in me and in my life. Jesus really made the difference for me!

## Analyzing the Faith Story

Notice the flow of the simple faith story or turn of events:

- ❊ The before

    *There was no account of a spiritual influence.*

- ❋ The change or search

    *The quest for peace became apparent.*
- ❋ The church connection

    *A friend extended an invitation to church.*
- ❋ The newfound joy!

    *The experience was pure joy.*
- ❋ New and real contentment

    *The experience was genuine peace.*
- ❋ Church involvement

    *Became involved in church activities.*
- ❋ New friendships

    *Have gained new peers and developed new friendships.*
- ❋ Co-workers witnessed change

    *Fellow employees noticed something positive was happening.*
- ❋ Your personal and strong unwavering faith!

    *Life has taken on a new meaning. I am moving in a new direction.*

## NOW WRITE YOUR OWN FAITH STORY BY FOLLOWING THE PREVIOUSLY GIVEN FORMAT

_____

_____

Once you have written your faith story, you will find that it will have a natural flow as you share it with others. The key is to share what God has done in *your* life. There will be people who will learn from your sharing and they will yearn for the peace. You will find that you *do* have a story to share. It doesn't have to be a long story but it will be meaningful because God has a purpose for it!

## EIGHT STEPS TO SOUL WINNING:

1. Love the Lord your God with all your heart.
2. Have a passion for lost souls.
3. Ask God to use you and fit you into His divine will.
4. Discover a person's spiritual weakness/need.
5. Act on that knowledge.
6. Befriend the person whom God places on your heart.
7. Follow up on your progress with that person.
8. Lead that person into the saving power of Christ.

## Go Out!!

Where will God send me? How can He use me? How can I approach people? What if I mess up? What if people laugh at me? What if fear overtakes me? What if I'm not convincing? What if? What if? What if?

You have your faith story planted in your heart and you're almost ready to be that spokesperson for Christ, but there still may be a little apprehension. Perhaps now you are fearful of the unknown. So were some of God's earliest messengers.

First Things First:

We are going to take a look at how certain Bible characters struggled with God's will to "Go Out" and be simple instruments of peace and love. Take notice of how God assured them and was willing to use and guide them just by being *who* they are.

### Lessons to Learn from Scripture

The Apostle Paul ministered to people with deep passion and his ministry was very fruitful. In contrast, before Paul became converted he was zealous to *destroy* the Christians, and went to great lengths to do so. Following his conversion, many people found it difficult to believe that he had actually changed, though he now had a deep passion to win souls for the Kingdom of God. He had been totally transformed by God's power. In 2 Corinthians 11:6 he says, "I may not be a trained speaker, but I do have knowledge." God called Paul to preach and to witness to the Gentiles.

In a similar way, God appointed Moses to lead the Israelites out of Egypt and out of the hands of Pharaoh. Moses was God's chosen instrument to lead his people out of slavery and into the Promised Land. God commanded Moses to go into Egypt to free God's people. Moses was surprised that God gave him this order.

He said, "Who am I, that I should go to Pharaoh and bring the Israelites out of Egypt?" (Exod 3:11).

Immediately Moses protested, saying, "What if they do not believe me or listen to me and say, 'The Lord did not appear to you?'" (Exod 4:1).

God then assured Moses that He was going to see him through by giving him authority and power to do His will. But that didn't really appease Moses. Once again Moses rebutted, saying that he had a speech impediment and pleaded that someone else be sent instead. The Lord told him his brother was already on his way to meet him; they would embark on the journey together (Exod 4:13). Isn't it just like God to provide the perfect solution? "You shall speak to him and put words in his mouth; I will help both of you speak and will teach you what to do" (Exod 4:15).

Moses questioned God; nevertheless, he was obedient. He met up with his brother Aaron and set out for Egypt. When they met up with God's people, Moses told them all what God had promised and they were very pleased to hear the good news that they were going to be free from slavery. Moses was up against some heavy battles and getting the people out was very difficult. He was up against Pharaoh the King of Egypt. He was a slave driver and when Moses attempted to plead with him, Pharaoh made God's people work harder. They were driven to make bricks and had to make a certain quota each day. Then God's people became full of doubt. The more that Moses continued to reassure God's promises to them, the more they disbelieved because they were being treated unfairly, and they were tired and wanted out of bondage. Again and again God reassured Moses that his people were going to be free.

God told Moses, "Therefore, say to the Israelites: 'I am the Lord, and I will bring you out from under the yoke of the Egyptians. I will free you from being slaves to them, and I will redeem you with an outstretched arm and with mighty acts of judgment. I will take you as my own people, and I will be your God. Then you will know that I am the Lord your God, who brought you out from under the yoke of the Egyptians. And I will bring you to the land I swore with uplifted hand to give to Abraham, to Isaac and to Jacob. I will give it to you as a possession. I am the Lord'" (Exod 6:6–8).

"Moses reported this to the Israelites, but they did not listen to him because of their discouragement and cruel bondage" (Exod 6:9). Then they became discouraged saying they were better off in misery. I wonder how we would have reacted if we were there at that point and time. On one hand we have all these promises given to us but then there is no sign of deliverance. But wait . . . God's promises never fail.

Such a promise in Proverbs says, "Many are the plans in a man's heart, but it is the Lord's purpose that prevails" (Prov 19:21). We can't always see the way before us, but God's purpose always prevails. When God makes a promise He will see it through. You see, God heard the moanings and groanings of His people, in other words God heard their prayers. And God had a plan and a way out for them. But most importantly, God wanted them to know that He was their God. *I am the Lord* . . . He remembered the promise and covenant that He made with them.

When the victory was won and the people were free, do you know what the people did? The people feared the Lord and put their trust in Him *and* in Moses His servant (Exod 14:31).

What can we learn from this story? When we undergo trials of any kind we must place our faith and trust in God. Remember this, He hears *our* moanings and groanings too. His promises are for us too! He is our God too! And we are his people! When freedom came there was singing and rejoicing with tambourines and dancing.

Moses's encouraging words should be for us also, as he told the people, "The Lord will fight for you; you need only to be still" (Exod 14:14). We don't see the way clearly in life but we know that God is the overseer. As Moses was leading God's people out of slavery and into safety, He provided water from the rock and food from heaven (Exod 17:5–6).

God understands frustration, God holds us up when we have little faith. Sometimes He tests our faith. Maybe we need to be still sometimes and wait a little longer for God to come to our rescue. Maybe God will send along a friend to give us encouragement just like He provided for Moses. Let's choose to believe in God's unfailing promises. Let's continue to moan and groan to Him. Let's see Him by faith, and let us believe that He is our Lord!

What did we learn from these studying the previous passages?

Perhaps we could ponder these conclusions:

- ✸ Soul winning isn't about being *trained* as a public speaker.
- ✸ Soul winning isn't about going it *alone*.
- ✸ Soul winning isn't about *thinking* you have to be perfect.
- ✸ Soul winning is about obedience to what God is saying to *you* personally.
- ✸ Soul winning is about trusting and allowing God to use *you*!
- ✸ Soul winning is about *availing* yourself of God's power to do what is required.

- ❈ Soul winning is *working* for God!
- ❈ Soul winning is *rescuing* God's people from darkness.
- ❈ Soul winning is *wise* and biblical.
- ❈ Soul winning is *passionate*.

Were Moses and Paul any different from you or me? Do we question or doubt God's authority? Are we fearful of building relationships for Christ?

Thought: *What if God's workers fully trusted in His unfailing power? What would soul winning be like? What would our churches be like?*

Take a moment to write your thoughts:

_____

_____

_____

_____

_____

_____

_____

_____

## Discovering the Whole Package

What do Christians believe? We believe that Jesus died for our sins; we believe that Jesus was raised to life again, and we learn that Jesus has a place for us to be with Him forever, in heaven. Heaven awaits the believer!

First Corinthians 15:20–22 says, "But Christ has indeed been raised from the dead, the firstfruits of those who have fallen asleep. For since death came through a man, the resurrection of the dead comes also through a man. For as in Adam we all die, so in Christ all will be made alive."

Jesus promised to provide the Holy Spirit in His absence until He returns for His children. Jesus promises to love His children always. When Jesus ascended back into heaven He did as promised; the Holy Spirit came to dwell among His people and they were comforted. How was that known? It was revealed in John 14:18–20, "I will not leave you as orphans; I will come to you. Before long the world will not see me anymore, but you will see me. Because I live, you also will live. On that day you will realize that I am in my Father and you are in me, and I am in you."

If, after studying these Scriptures you do not feel comfortable or prepared to launch out into the open field to proclaim the Gospel, learn from Paul's example when he wrote to the church in Corinth: "When I came to you, brothers, I did not come with eloquence or superior wisdom as I proclaimed to you the testimony about God. For I resolved to know nothing while I was with you except Jesus Christ and Him crucified. I came to you in weakness and fear, and with much trembling. My message and my preaching were not with wise and persuasive words, but with the demonstration of the Spirit's power so that your faith may not rest on men's wisdom but on God's power" (1 Cor 2:1–5).

How did Paul display humility in the above passage?

_____

_____

_____

_____

_____

_____

_____

_____

_____

_____

_____

_____

_____

## THE BELIEVER'S COMMITMENT

> *"Therefore since Christ suffered in His body, arm yourselves also with the same attitude, because he who has suffered in his body is done with sin! As a result, he does not live the rest of his earthly life for evil human desires, but rather for the will of God"* (1 Pet 4:1-2).

That sounds like a plan. God's plan is for His children to be like Christ. *We are done with sinning, and are now living out the will of God for the rest of our earthly lives!* Isn't that the believer's commitment? To be done with sinning? *Can we really be like Christ?*

Read Philippians 2:1-11 to help you answer the questions below.

What is developed from being united with Christ? (vv. 1-4)

_____

_____

_____

_____

What type of attitude should we have? (vv. 6-11)

_____

_____

_____

_____

What then, should the believer's commitment be? Summarize.

_____

_____

_____

_____

The Samaritan woman who met Jesus at the well had just come to know Him and, as a result of her *testimony,* many of the Samaritans from that town became believers. You see; Christians are to *be the Good News* before they *share the Good News.* Jesus stayed two days with the people there and many more became believers (John 4:40–41). They said to this woman, "We no longer believe just because of what you said; now we have heard for ourselves, and we know that this man really is the Savior of the world" (John 4:42).

How did so many Samaritans become seekers and believers?

_____

_____

_____

_____

_____

Have you become the "*Good News*" in your neighborhood? How can you set an example? (Read v. 42)

_____

_____

_____

_____

As people everywhere share the Good News of Christ, many people place their faith in Jesus and become believers. One example is the royal official's son, who laid deathly ill. The royal official's son was very close to death when he asked Jesus to come to his son before he died. Jesus told him that his son would live, so the man took Jesus at His word and left. As a result of this miracle, his entire household believed (John 4:49–50).

Jesus gave an open invitation to come to Him. It was at the last and greatest day of the feast. "Jesus stood and said in a loud voice, 'If anyone is thirsty, let him come to me and drink, whoever believes in me as the Scriptures has said, streams of living water will flow from within him'" (John 7:37–38).

So, in preparation for fieldwork, remember not to depend on yourself, but rely on God's power. He is the One who provides strength for the evangelistic journey out into the streets, the malls, the community centers, and the coffee shops. The entire fields are ripe for harvest to bring souls home for Him! It is His work that must be fulfilled! And He will always walk beside you as long as you are willing to be used by Him and as long as you are obedient to go where he sends you.

May God bless you in a mighty way to help restore the lost and the broken to His safekeeping. Only God's power can bring about the renewing of the mind, the transformation of the heart and soul, to become believers in Christ.

"For the message of the cross is foolishness to those who are perishing, but to us who are being saved it is the power of God" (1 Cor 1:18). May God work through you and give you strength and joy as you labor for Him!

The following Friendship Evangelism Progress Chart was designed to support *you* as the newly trained evangelist. The "8 C's of Evangelism" included in the chart serve as a reminder of what you have learned as you keep an account of those whom God places in your heart, to pray for, and to encourage him/her into the saving knowledge of Jesus Christ. May you be blessed and enjoy the journey of faith and discover that soul winning is not complicated, it is rewarding! Place the names of those you will be praying for on the left and place a "check" on each category as you progress and build your ongoing relationship with that person. The action that you take does not necessarily have to be in this order. Each step will be victorious!

## Friendship Evangelism Progress Chart
### The Eight C's

| Name: | 1 | 2 | 3 | 4 | 5 | 6 | 7 | 8 |
|---|---|---|---|---|---|---|---|---|
| | | | | | | | | |
| | | | | | | | | |
| | | | | | | | | |
| | | | | | | | | |
| | | | | | | | | |
| | | | | | | | | |
| | | | | | | | | |

Key: √
1. Initial Contact
2. Initial Conversation
3. Community Interaction
4. Church Invitation
5. Communicated Faith Story
6. Confidence Building
7. Challenged to Seek the Lord
8. Commitment Made

The target of your evangelism outreach is to focus on certain people. Perhaps God has already placed those people in your path to befriend. Why not choose four people to pray for on a regular basis and allow God to work through you to help them along the journey of following Christ? You may choose a family member or a co-worker or your librarian. Remember as you pray the prayer pledge, to wait upon God to be your guide through the process. It will not be an overnight process; relationships take time to build.

Don't forget to give God the praise and glory for your successes!

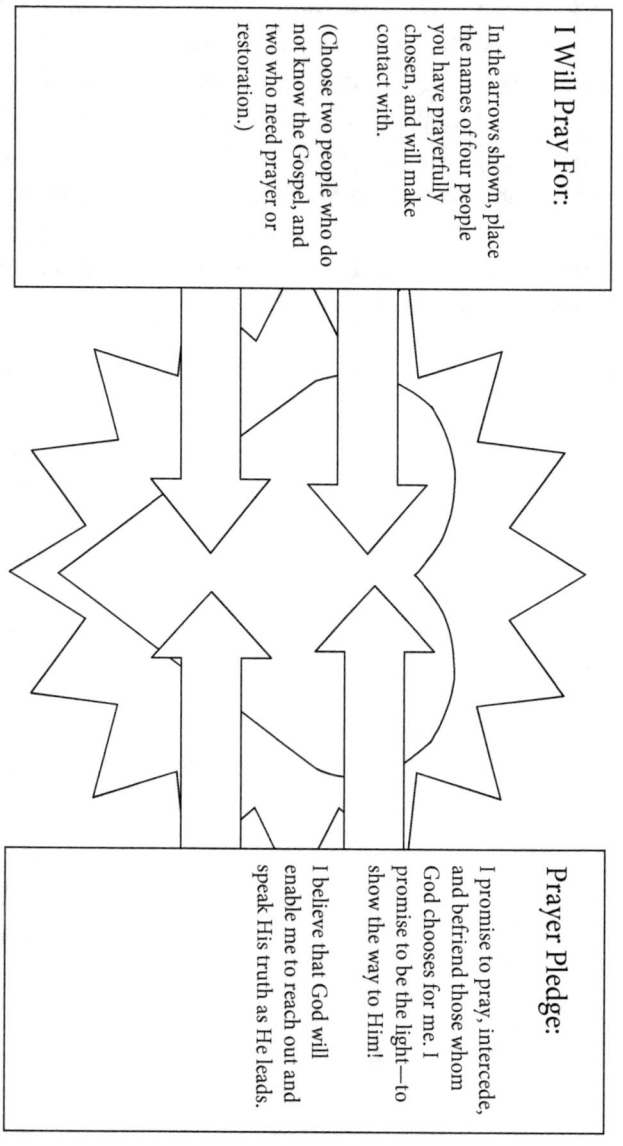

www.ingramcontent.com/pod-product-compliance
Lightning Source LLC
LaVergne TN
LVHW021620080426
835510LV00019B/2670